This book belongs to:

_____

_____

_____

Morocco is a country in the northwest of Africa. Its official name is the Kingdom of Morocco. It borders Algeria to the east and southeast and Mauritania to the south.

The Mediterranean Sea is located to the north of Morocco and the Atlantic Ocean is located to the west.

The Moroccan flag features a green, five-pointed star (a pentagram). The star symbolises the five pillars of Islam, while the red represents the blood of the ancestors.

Toubkal Mountain, situated within the Atlas Mountains, stands as the highest peak in North Africa, reaching a height of 4165 metres.

The Amazigh flag comprises bands of blue, green, and yellow, symbolising the sea, nature, and desert, respectively. At its centre, the red yaz symbolises the "free man," reflecting the meaning of the Berber word Amazigh.

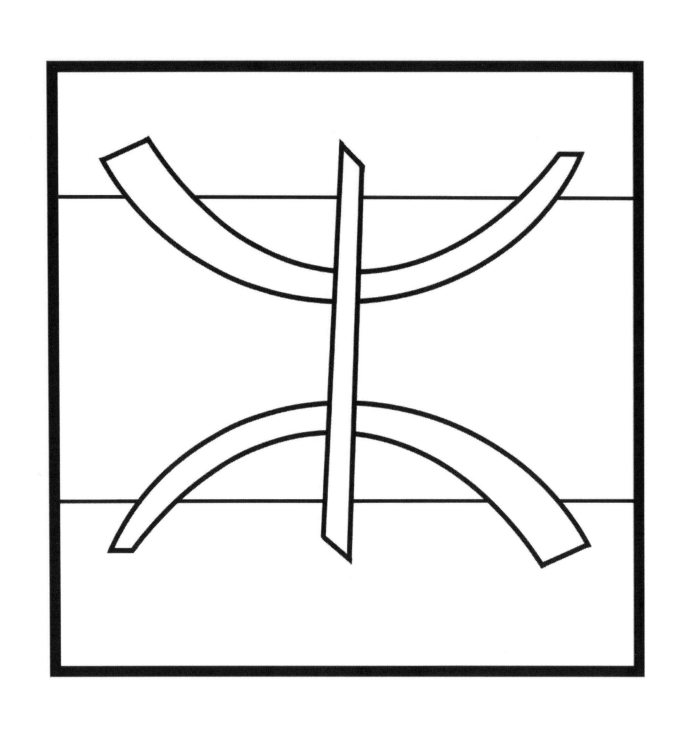

The Atlas lion, also known as the North African lion, denotes an extinct population of the lion subspecies Panthera leo leo. It inhabited the mountains and deserts of the Maghreb of North Africa, stretching from Morocco to Egypt.

The argan tree is renowned for the numerous health benefits it offers, and it exclusively thrives in the southwest of Morocco. Moroccans utilize its fruit to produce high-quality oil.

The predominant religion in Morocco is Islam. Islam is founded on belief in a single God (Allah), faith in Muhammad (Allah's prophet), and belief in the Quran (Allah's revealed book).

Moroccan architecture has been shaped by numerous influences over millennia. Elements from Arab culture, Spain, Portugal, and France, alongside religious inspirations, have amalgamated to create a diverse array of styles.

Volubilis is situated in Morocco, 31 km from the city of Meknes, and a short distance from the city of Moulay Idris. The term originates from Latin and translates to "generous." The site is adorned with captivating ruins adorned with exquisite mosaics and vibrant tiles illustrating Roman mythology.

The primary purpose of the city walls was to defend cities from potential invaders and attacks. The walls and gates served as protective barriers, and they were strategically designed to make it difficult for enemies to breach the city.

The term Kasbah refers to a city built inside high defensive walls. The building is made of mud and soil and is designed to last and stand strong against intruders' attacks.

A Moroccan Riad is a building found primarily in Old Medinas, characterized by an interior garden/courtyard with individual private rooms around it. Riads usually have a minimalistic outside, with very little windows.

In the centre of the Riad, there is a fountain, lavishly adorned with zellige tiles and intricately carved plaster. It is encompassed by four distinct gardens, featuring lemon, fig, mint, and various other trees.

The term "Zellige" in Arabic translates to "polished stone" or "tile". This artisanal tradition originated in Morocco during the 10th century and rapidly disseminated worldwide, largely due to the Spanish invasion.

Hassan Tower is a historic minaret of an incomplete mosque located in the heart of the Moroccan city of Rabat. The minaret was built during the reign of Almohad Caliph Abu Yusuf Yaqub al-Mansur in the 12th century AD during the construction of the Hassan Mosque, which was considered one of the largest mosques in that period. But this construction stopped after the death of the Sultan in 1199.

The Blue Gate is a historical landmark in the city of Fes, Morocco. It was built in the late 12th century and is one of the most iconic structures in the city.

Zellige tiles remain a staple of Moroccan culture and art decoration. Since their invention, they have been a symbol of sophistication, wealth, and power for royal and religious establishments.

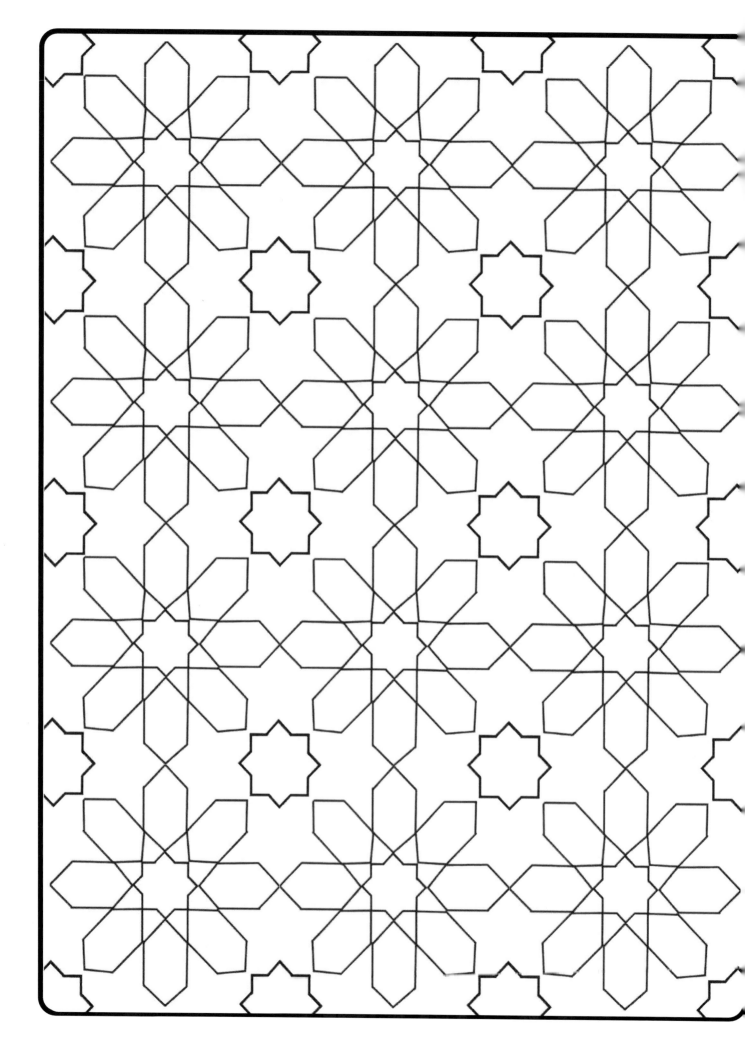

The Moroccan balcony is an elegant and exotic addition to any outdoor space. The characteristics of Moroccan balconies can be seen in their patterns and textures, for example Arabic patterns, bright textiles, floor pillows and fantastic lanterns.

Moroccan ceramic tiles have their origins in the Islamic religion and Muslim traditions. The complexity of these patterns is believed to have stemmed from the strict Muslim laws that artists had to follow. Since in the Islam religion they were forbidden to paint living figures, they painted shapes and line work instead.

Chefchaouen is a small town in Morocco with a rich history. Nestled in the Rif mountains, this old town is known for its beautiful surroundings and architecture, but what makes it stand out are the striking and varying shades of blue walls. it is one of The Most Colorful Cities Around The World.

The creation of Zellij is a meticulous process that requires exceptional craftsmanship. Skilled artisans, known as Maalems, meticulously cut and shape small pieces of ceramic tiles or colored stones to create intricate patterns.

Surrounded by a vast palm grove, the medina in Marrakech is called the "red city" because of its buildings and ramparts of beaten clay, which were built during the residence of the Almohads. The heart of the medina is Jamaa el-Fna square, a vibrant marketplace.

The geometric patterns in Zellij hold symbolic significance in Moroccan culture. Each pattern has its meaning, representing elements from nature, spirituality, and Islamic symbolism. From stars and rosettes to arabesques and calligraphic inscriptions, Zellij patterns evoke a sense of harmony, balance, and divine order.

The old medina of Fez is considered the oldest city in Morocco. Fez is one of Morocco's four imperial cities and was once the capital of Morocco.

Zellige can be found all over Morocco, from private homes to water fountains to mosques.

Water fountains are also common in the Medina. In the past, there was no running water and it was the only place where its inhabitants obtained their supplies. The fountain consists of zellij tiles covering its walls and basins, along with brass spigots for dispensing water.

Al-Qarawiyyin is a mosque and university in Fez, Morocco. The initial mosque, built by Fatima Al-Fihri in 859AD, later became home to the world's first degree-issuing institution, hosting classes not only on the Islamic sciences but mathematics, science, astronomy, and foreign languages as well.

The Tagine is a traditional Moroccan meal made in a pottery dish, also known as a tagine. It is a stew that can include meat and vegetables cooked in a special pot.

Couscous is a small steamed ball of wheat, often mixed with vegetables and spices. While it is the traditional Friday dish, couscous is also served during baptisms and wedding celebrations.

Mint tea is shared after most meals. it is usually served very sweet, with sugar chipped off a sugarloaf. Moroccans enjoy drinking mint tea sweetened with sugar. The people take their time making tea and sipping it with family and guests.

Briouats are stuffed pastry triangles that taste rich in the inside. There are basically two categories of briouats: sweet and salty. Sweet briouats are stuffed with almond or peanut paste mixed with orange flower water. After they're deep-fried, they're dipped in honey.
Salty briouats are bigger in size. They're stuffed with seafood, chicken, or ground red meat.

Named after the pot it is cooked in, tangia is a traditional Moroccan specialty, a beef dish slow-cooked in the embers of wood fires.

Generally, traditional clothing for women and men in Morocco consists mostly of long robes with hoods and traditional slippers.

the Moroccan Caftan. It is a long flowy dress decorated with all kinds of embroidery designs and sequin colors, reserved for formal events, celebrations, and holidays.

The Selham is a traditional Moroccan garment that is steeped in history and culture. It is a large, long or mid-length cape that is typically adorned with a hood and tassel.

Sahrawi (south) women wear
the Melhfa to protect themselves
from the blowing sands caused by
rough winds in the desert.

Jabador is a traditional Moroccan outfit worn on various occasions . It's a set composed of three pieces: A pair of pants. A tunic. A vest.

Women in some parts of Morocco also wear up what is called the Haik, which is a traditional white full body dress that is made of silk and wool. The Haik covers the whole body except face and hands and it is mainly used in cold and conservative areas in Morocco. The Haik in this case serves both the purposes of modesty and of protection from harsh weather.

Tazerzit is a silver fibula. This piece of jewelry was worn in the past by women as a form of adornment. This item of jewelry was mostly worn in daily life or for special occasions such as weddings.

In the south region of Morocco, women and girls wear clothes belonging to each tribe and village. This way, people of the region can distinguish the woman's tribe by her clothing. This applies both to daily clothing or special occasion attire.

Unlike the Caftan, which is one-piece dress, Takchita is a Moroccan traditional dress that is composed of two parts, the first layer is called Takchita and the second one is called Dfina.

The Cheich is a large indigo-dyed cotton fabric used to tie around the head of men from the desert worn in their day to day life, to serve as shield from wind-borne sand.

The fez hat is a conical man's headdress and handmade felted with natural wool. Its name comes from the city of Fez in Morocco. It is one of the typical accessories of traditional Moroccan clothing. Men usually wear it during special religious celebrations like Eids.

This traditional Moroccan leather shoe is the most worn in Morocco and is an essential accessory for religious ceremonies and festivals.

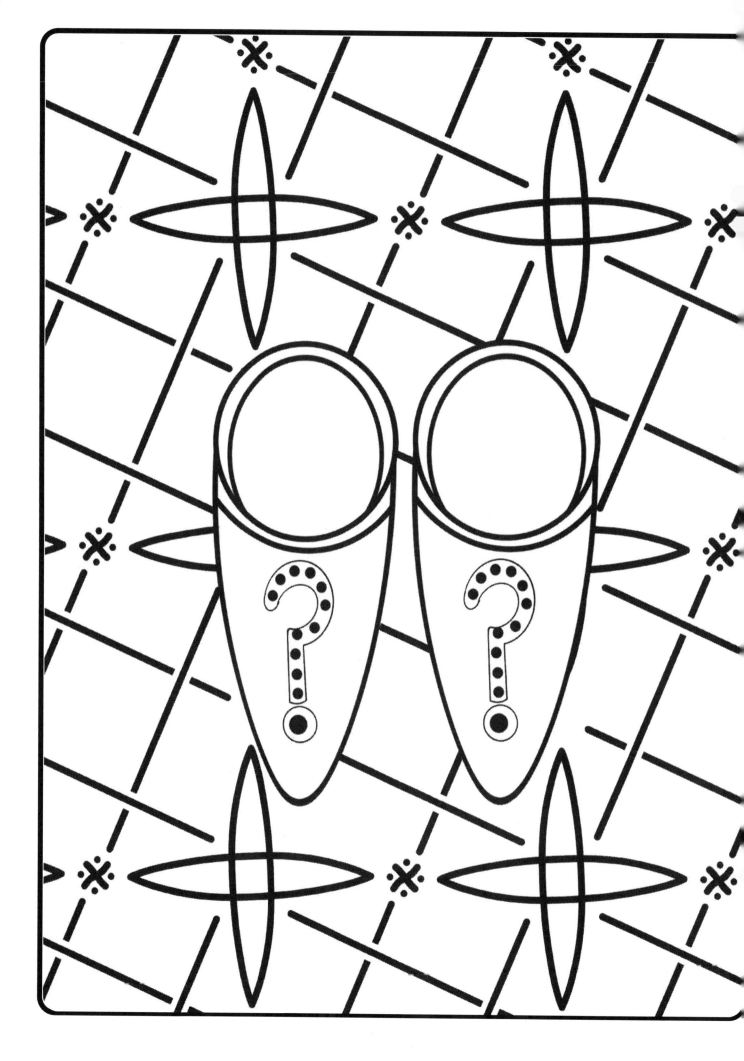

Also known as Moroccan Halloween, the Boujloud Festival takes place a few days after Eid al-Adha. It involves people wearing sheepskin, goatskin, or bird feathers. After dressing up, the participants, accompanied by flute players, drummers and large crowds of people, move to the most famous squares in their respective cities for street shows.

Held annually in El Kelaa M'Gouna, approximately 50 miles northeast of Ouarzazate, in the Dades Valley, Morocco's Festival of Roses celebrates the season's rose harvest. Various activities are held during the festival. Streets are covered with blankets of roses, Berber groups outdoors concerts, flower shows, etc. The last day of the festival is the day to elect Miss Roses. The most beautiful women come out to dance dressed in their best caftans and decorated with roses.

Gnawa music is probably the most spiritual and enchanting music you can find in Morocco, originating from the black people brought to Morocco for the slave trade. Later on, after Islam came to Morocco bringing with it their freedom, they dedicated their music to thank God and turned it into spiritual religious chants.

Women used the henna plant, which grows in the Mediterranean area, to make a thick paste mix of crushed leaves and water. They used it to tattoo their skin with unique designs and symbols that distinguished Amazigh women from one tribe to another.

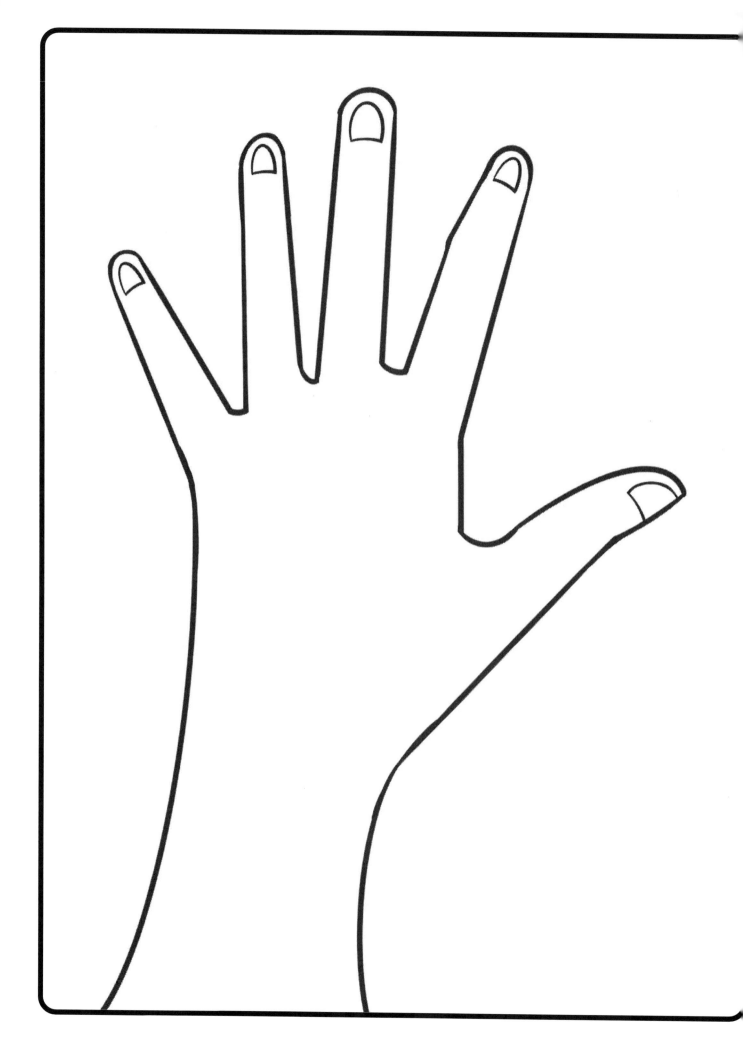

The traditional Moroccan wedding is full of fascinating customs and elaborate processes, from the henna party to the wedding food. Certainly, the most enchanting element is the wedding dresses a bride in Morocco will choose.

Lebsa lfasiya is the traditional dress from the Fez region, also called "ebsa lekbira" (the great outfit). Its large size and shape, along with the accompanying elaborate jewellery, characterise this type of wedding dress. It can be white, red, or green.

Fantasia is a traditional exhibition of horsemanship in Morocco performed during cultural festivals and to close Moroccan wedding celebrations.

Made in United States
Orlando, FL
01 December 2024

54758805R00059